I0824401

PENN STATE NITTANY LIONS

BY

GORDON OWENS

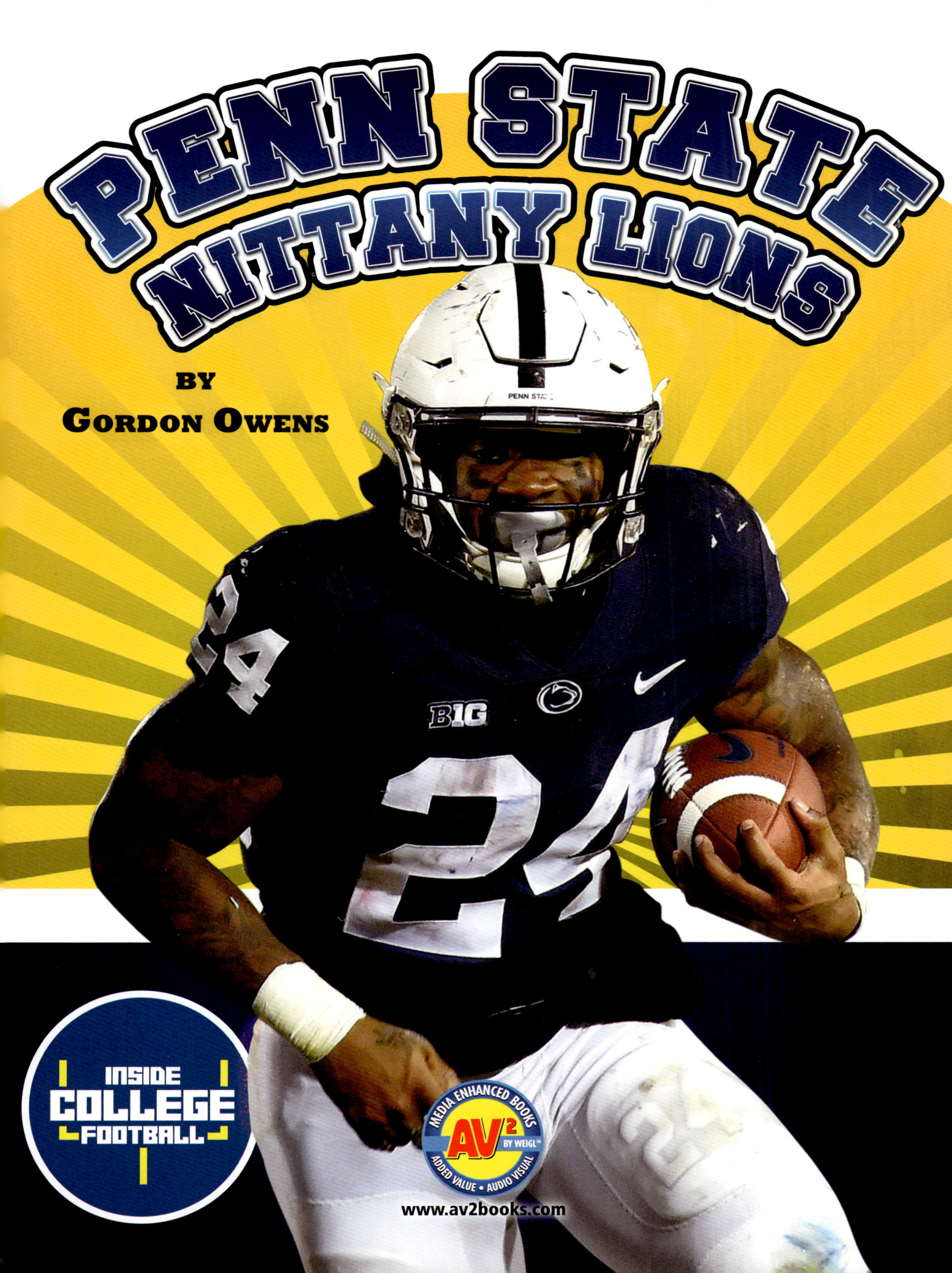

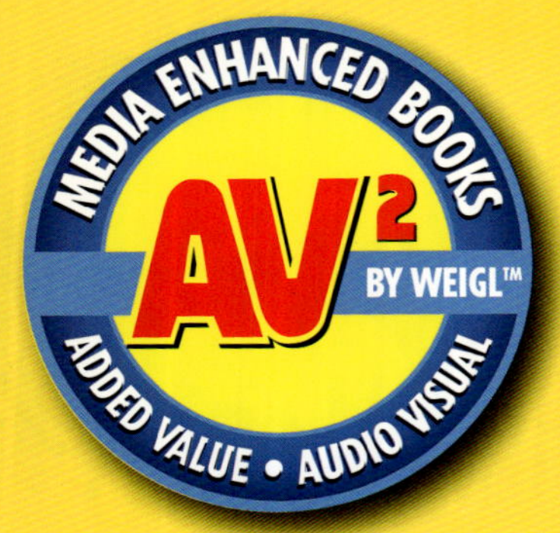

Go to **www.av2books.com,** and enter this book's unique code.

BOOK CODE

AVR57935

AV² by Weigl brings you media enhanced books that support active learning.

AV² provides enriched content that supplements and complements this book. Weigl's AV² books strive to create inspired learning and engage young minds in a total learning experience.

Your AV² Media Enhanced books come alive with...

Audio
Listen to sections of the book read aloud.

Key Words
Study vocabulary, and complete a matching word activity.

Video
Watch informative video clips.

Quizzes
Test your knowledge.

Embedded Weblinks
Gain additional information for research.

Slideshow
View images and captions, and prepare a presentation.

Try This!
Complete activities and hands-on experiments.

... and much, much more!

Published by AV² by Weigl
350 5th Avenue, 59th Floor
New York, NY 10118
Website: www.av2books.com

Library of Congress Control Number: 2018968211

ISBN 978-1-7911-0081-0 (hardcover)
ISBN 978-1-7911-0082-7 (multi-user eBook)
ISBN 978-1-7911-0083-4 (single-user eBook)

Printed in Guangzhou, China
1 2 3 4 5 6 7 8 9 0 23 22 21 20 19

042019
102318

Project Coordinator: Jared Siemens   Designer: Terry Paulhus

Every reasonable effort has been made to trace ownership and to obtain permission to reprint copyright material. The publishers would be pleased to have any errors or omissions brought to their attention so that they may be corrected in subsequent printings.

The publisher acknowledges Alamy, Getty Images, and Wikimedia Commons as its primary image suppliers for this title.

Penn State Nittany Lions

CONTENTS

Introduction

The Pennsylvania State University Nittany Lions have been playing football for more than 100 years. They have had their ups and downs over the years, but they have become a top team, winning National Championships and bowl games. Their student athletes continue to lead the school to football victory.

One of Penn State's biggest **rivals** is the University of Minnesota. Penn's first game as part of the Big Ten Conference was against Minnesota's Golden Gophers. The Nittany Lions won 38–20. The University of Pittsburgh Panthers and the Michigan State University Spartans are also big rivals of the Nittany Lions.

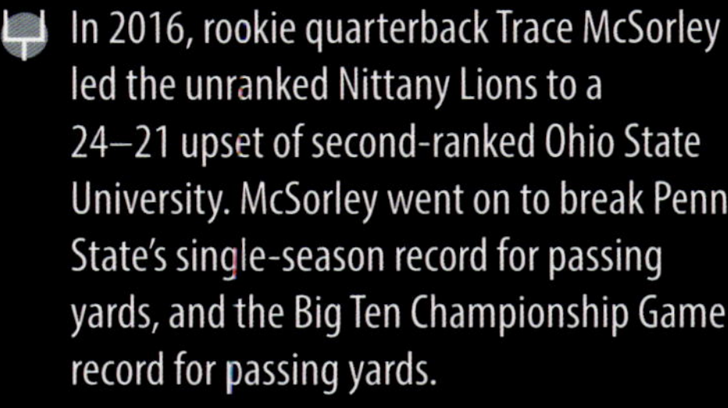

In 2016, rookie quarterback Trace McSorley led the unranked Nittany Lions to a 24–21 upset of second-ranked Ohio State University. McSorley went on to break Penn State's single-season record for passing yards, and the Big Ten Championship Game record for passing yards.

There are many Penn State fans who attend all the games and root loudly for the team. One of the biggest fan **traditions** at Penn State's home of Beaver Stadium is called a "White House" game. Every fan in Beaver Stadium wears a white shirt. The stadium has hosted one White House game almost every season since 2004.

Jahan Dotson was the first true freshman to start a game at Penn State since 2014. The wide receiver had 13 receptions in the 2018 season.

PENN STATE

Stadium Beaver Stadium

Division Big Ten East

Head Coach James Franklin

Location University Park, Pennsylvania

National Championships 2

Nicknames Blue & White, Nittanymen

4
Conference Championships

49
Bowls Played

125
Seasons

31
Lambert-Meadowlands Trophies

History

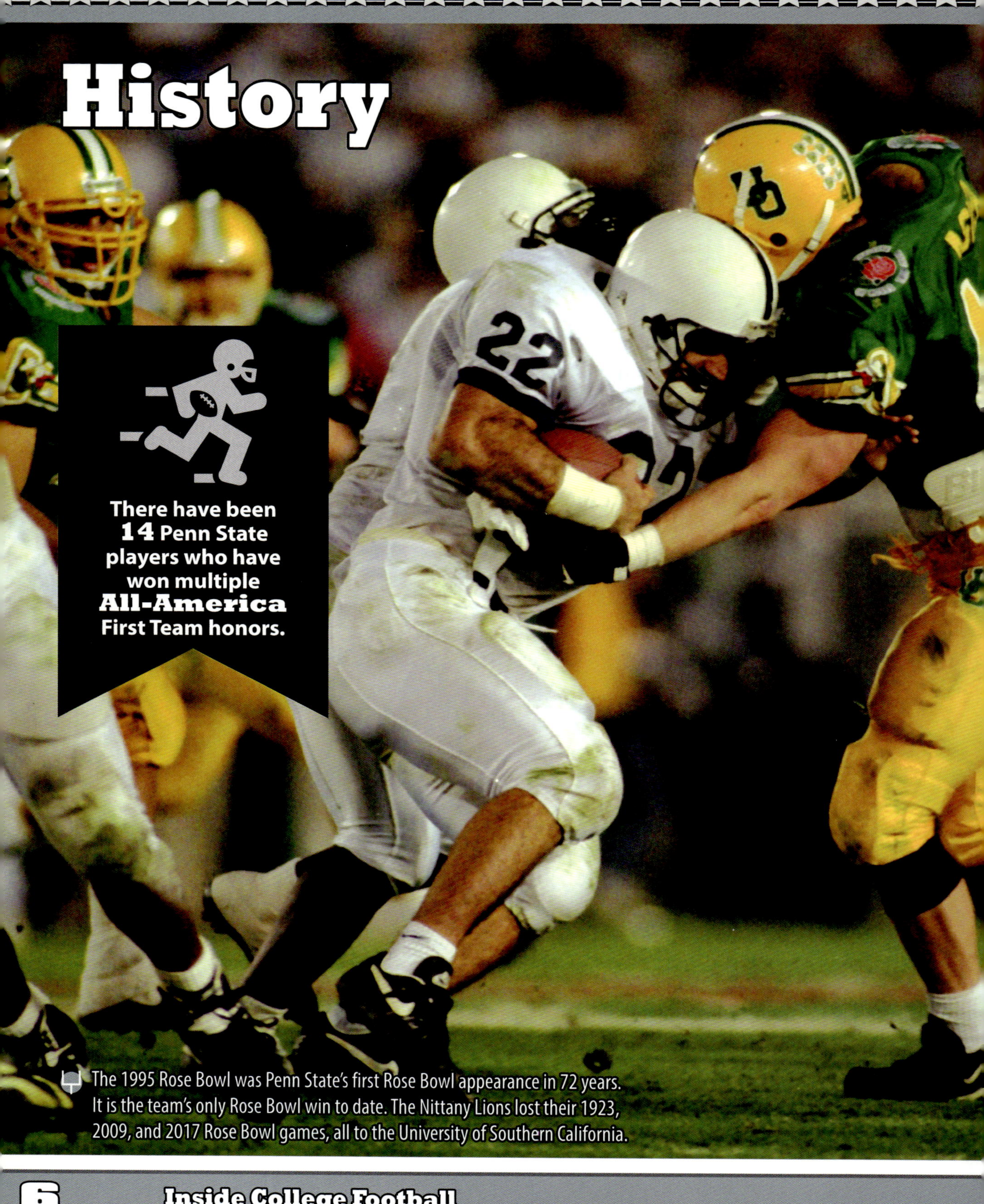

There have been **14** Penn State players who have won multiple **All-America** First Team honors.

The 1995 Rose Bowl was Penn State's first Rose Bowl appearance in 72 years. It is the team's only Rose Bowl win to date. The Nittany Lions lost their 1923, 2009, and 2017 Rose Bowl games, all to the University of Southern California.

Penn State football began in 1887. The team played its first game on November 12, 1887, against Bucknell University, and won 54–0. Bucknell demanded a rematch, and Penn State won again, 24–0. For the first five years, Penn State played without a head coach. In 1892, player George Hoskins stepped up as the team's leader. Even though he was a player at the time, he became the head coach. Hoskins coached for five years, and in 1894, he had his first undefeated season.

For a long time, Penn State played as an independent team. In 1990, the National Collegiate Athletic Association (NCAA) asked Penn State to join the Big Ten Conference, and it became a Division 1 team. The Nittany Lions played their first NCAA game in 1993. Their 1994 season was very successful. They went the whole year undefeated and won their first conference championship. They even defeated the University of Oregon Ducks 38–20 in the Rose Bowl at the end of that season.

After years of difficult seasons, James Franklin became the Nittany Lions' head coach in 2014. In 2016, Penn State won the Big Ten Conference championship for the fourth time. That same year, Penn State was ranked in the Associated Press Top 25 Poll for the first time since 2011.

Nine coaches led the Nittany Lions from 1887 to 1917. Many of Penn State's early teams won 60 percent or more of their games. The 1912 team had a perfect season, going 8–0–0 under Coach Bill Hollenback.

The Stadium

Beaver Stadium is consistently voted one of the best football stadiums in the country and was ranked the number-one stadium in college football in 2016.

Penn State's first field was called Beaver Field. The first game was played there on November 6, 1893, and Penn State won 32–0. There were only 500 seats at Beaver Field. In 1909, Penn State opened New Beaver Field. New Beaver Field had 30,000 seats and was made of wood. It also housed fields for many other sports, including baseball, **lacrosse**, and soccer. In 1936, New Beaver Field was torn down and rebuilt with steel.

In 1960, Penn State decided to build a new stadium. However, the university wanted to keep part of its old stadium. New Beaver Field was dismantled into 700 pieces. The pieces were moved 1 mile (1.6 kilometers) east, and the university started building again. This time, Penn State added another 16,000 seats.

Today, Beaver Stadium is one of the largest football stadiums in the world. Since the stadium was rebuilt in 1960, Penn State has expanded it several times. In 1984, lights were added. More recently, the university installed video screens and skyboxes. Beaver Stadium is more than twice its original size and can seat more than 100,000 people. It is the second-largest stadium in college football.

Because Penn State used pieces of its original stadium each time it renovated or constructed a new stadium, parts of the original 1909 New Beaver Field are still in use at Beaver Stadium.

Where They Play

Welcome to Beaver Stadium. Die-hard fans turn out rain or shine to cheer on their team. For more than a century, Nittany Lions fans have packed the stadium for home football games. A winning team, a top marching band, and many fan traditions make Beaver Stadium one of college football's best.

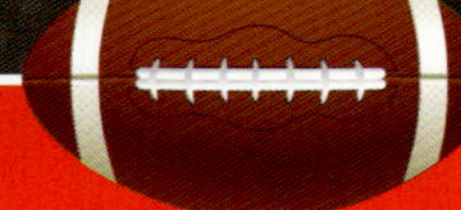

BIG TEN WEST

1. **Northwestern University**
   Evanston, Illinois
2. **Purdue University**
   West Lafayette, Indiana
3. **University of Illinois**
   Urbana-Champaign, Illinois
4. **University of Iowa**
   Iowa City, Iowa
5. **University of Minnesota**
   Minneapolis, Minnesota
6. **University of Nebraska**
   Lincoln, Nebraska
7. **University of Wisconsin**
   Madison, Wisconsin

Arena
Beaver Stadium

Location
University Park, Pennsylvania

Broke Ground
1959

Completed
September 17, 1960 (opening day)

Surface
Real Grass

Features
- Seating capacity of 106,572
- Trophies are on display in the Pepsi Fan Zone of the stadium
- Named after Pennsylvania governor James A. Beaver

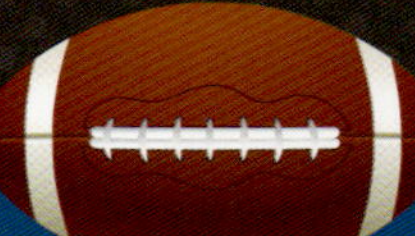

BIG TEN EAST

1. **Indiana University**
   Bloomington, Indiana
2. **Michigan State University**
   East Lansing, Michigan
3. **Ohio State University**
   Columbus, Ohio
4. ★ **Pennsylvania State University**
   State College, Pennsylvania
5. **Rutgers University–New Brunswick**
   New Brunswick–Piscataway, New Jersey
6. **University of Maryland**
   College Park, Maryland
7. **University of Michigan**
   Ann Arbor, Michigan

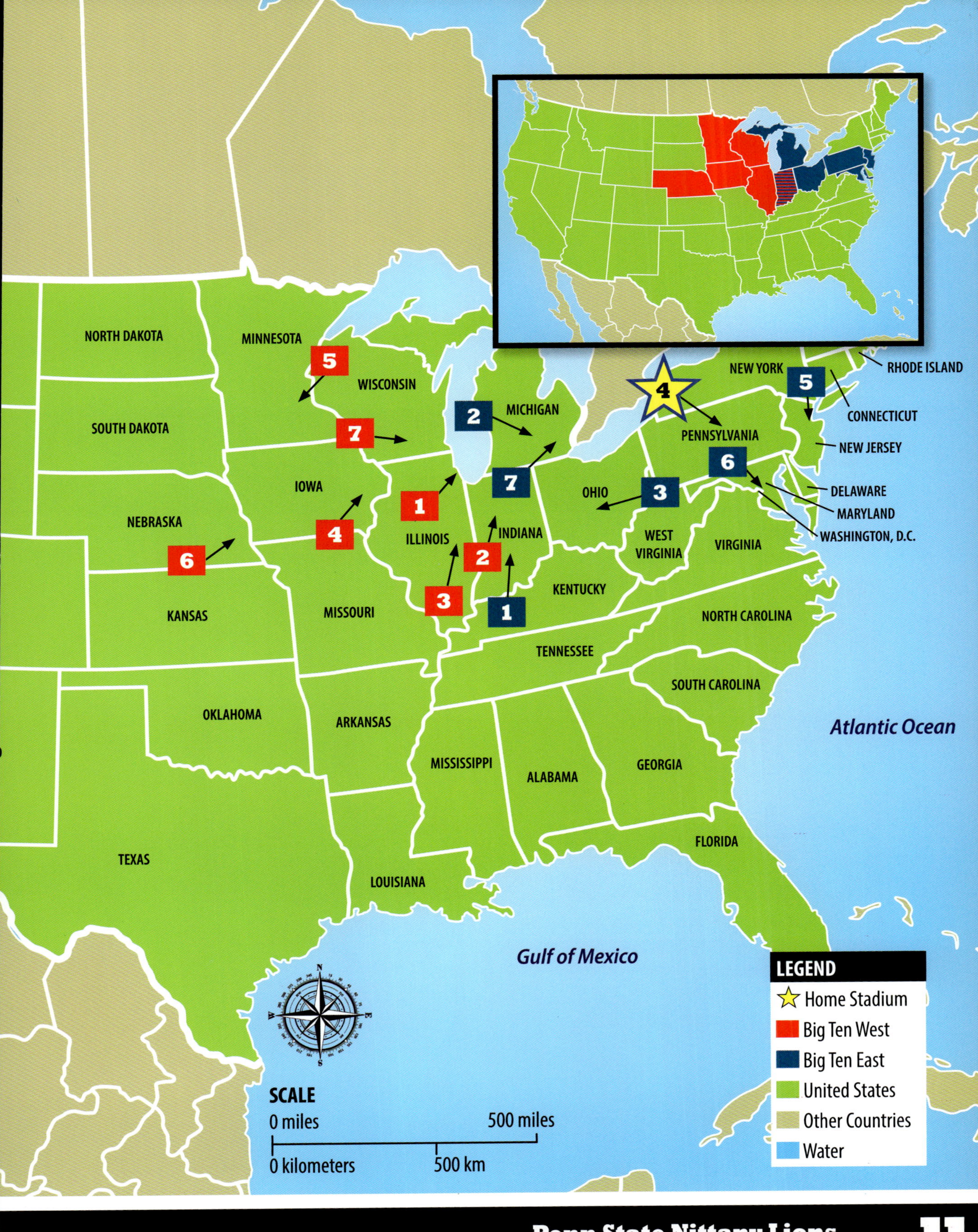
NORTH DAKOTA
SOUTH DAKOTA
NEBRASKA
KANSAS
OKLAHOMA
TEXAS
MINNESOTA
IOWA
MISSOURI
ARKANSAS
LOUISIANA
WISCONSIN
ILLINOIS
MICHIGAN
INDIANA
OHIO
KENTUCKY
TENNESSEE
MISSISSIPPI
ALABAMA
GEORGIA
FLORIDA
SOUTH CAROLINA
NORTH CAROLINA
VIRGINIA
WEST VIRGINIA
PENNSYLVANIA
NEW YORK
NEW JERSEY
CONNECTICUT
RHODE ISLAND
DELAWARE
MARYLAND
WASHINGTON, D.C.
Atlantic Ocean
Gulf of Mexico
SCALE
0 miles
500 miles
0 kilometers
500 km
LEGEND
Home Stadium
Big Ten West
Big Ten East
United States
Other Countries
Water

The Uniforms

The Nittany Lions' **Generation of Greatness** helmets are the only Penn State helmets that have player **numbers** painted on them.

- Penn State auctioned off many "Generations of Greatness" jerseys. Some jerseys sold for thousands of dollars. All proceeds went to the university's athletic department.

When the team first started playing, the players wore no padding, just knee-length pants and canvas jackets. In the 1880s, the school colors were pink and black. Because pink faded to white in the sun, the colors were officially changed to blue and white in March 1890. The Lions' home jerseys are usually all blue with white accents and numbers. Their away jerseys are white with blue accents and numbers. Both are worn with white pants.

AWAY

The Nittany Lions sometimes wear special alternate uniforms. In 2017, Penn State introduced a uniform called "Generations of Greatness." The uniform used various elements of past uniforms and was only worn for a single game. The jersey had a white stripe on the sleeve and a blue stripe on the pants. It also had white cleats and a gray face mask. These details were all pulled from many different times in the team's past to honor and celebrate Penn State's century of tradition.

The Nittany Lions do not use merit stickers or any other helmet decals on their plain white helmets, but have agreed to place a bowl decal on their helmets each time they play in a bowl game since the 1997 Fiesta Bowl.

Student Athletes

In the spring of 2018, the average **grade point average** (GPA) of student athletes at Penn State was **3.15** out of a possible **4**.

In addition to attending the Rose Bowl, Penn State athletes also claimed nine conference titles during the 2016–17 school year. Penn State student athletes also served more than 6,200 hours of community service.

Being a college student athlete is hard work. Student athletes have to perform well on the football field and in the classroom. Penn State student athletes are required to meet a minimum grade point average and attend all of their classes. Penn State student athletes also have access to the Morgan Academic Support Center. Penn State offers many other services to help students balance academic and athletic life.

Many student athletes are given athletic scholarships. An athletic scholarship is a financial aid agreement between the athlete and their college or university. Athletes who do not receive an athletic scholarship can be "walk-on" members of the team. This means they are on the team, but without athletic financial aid. Penn State typically awards the maximum number of football scholarships allowed, which is 85.

Student athlete KJ Hamler started at Penn State in 2018 as a freshman wide receiver majoring in journalism. Hamler is one of Penn State's 85 football scholarship recipients for the season.

Bowl Games

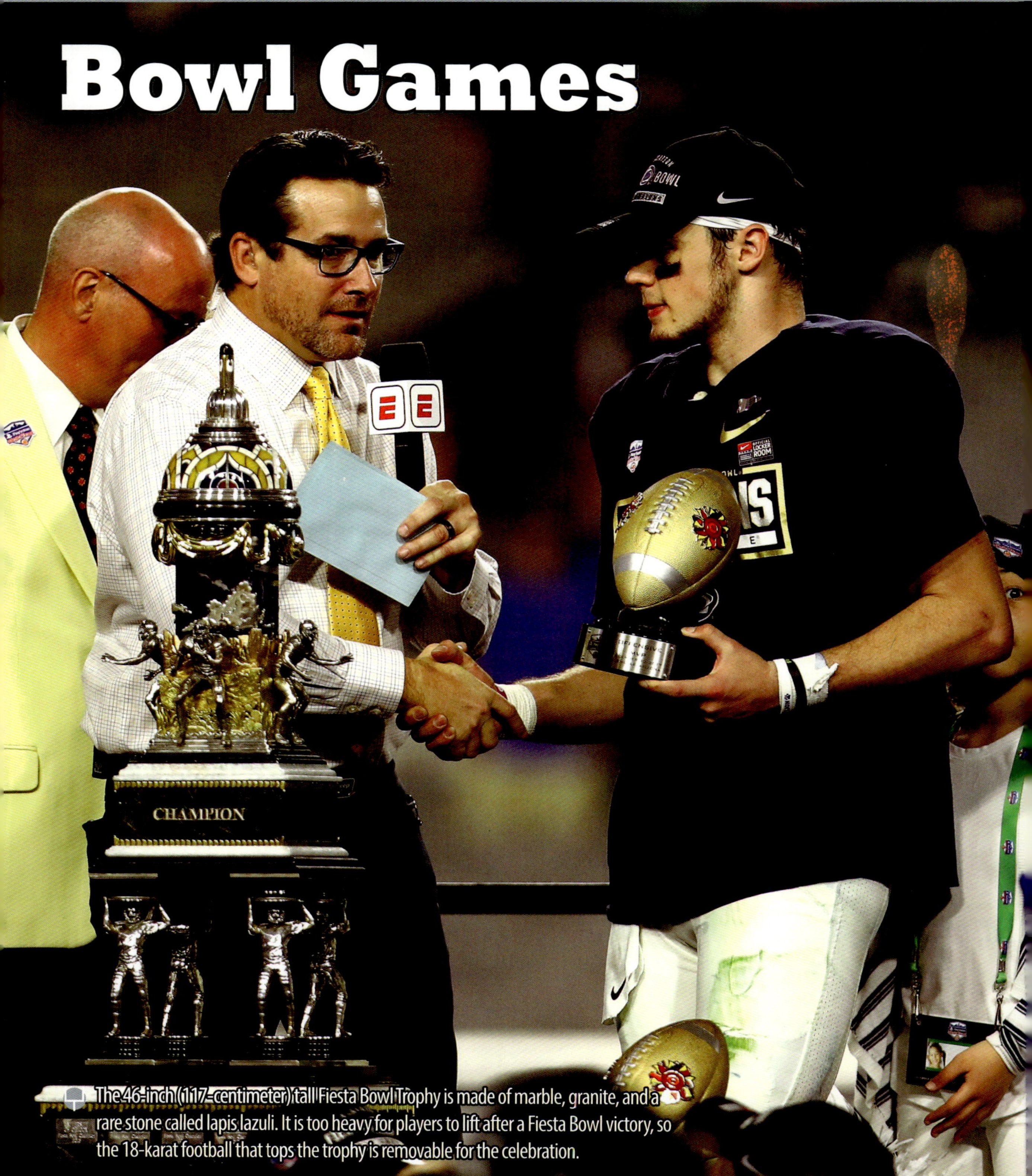

The 46-inch (117-centimeter) tall Fiesta Bowl Trophy is made of marble, granite, and a rare stone called lapis lazuli. It is too heavy for players to lift after a Fiesta Bowl victory, so the 18-karat football that tops the trophy is removable for the celebration.

After the college football season ends, a rare sports tradition begins. There is no NCAA-sponsored **postseason** for the sport of football. Instead, a variety of games called bowl games are played. There are currently 40 bowl games played between college football teams. These games give teams the chance to play rivals or new teams. It is also a chance to compete for respect and wins even after teams have finished with the regular season.

Penn State played its first bowl game on January 1, 1923, at the Rose Bowl. The Nittany Lions lost to the University of Southern California 14–3. The team has been to the Rose Bowl a total of four times and has won 29 of its 49 bowl games.

Penn State played in the 2017 Fiesta Bowl on December 30 against Washington State University. Both the **Offensive** Player of the Game award and the **Defensive** Player of the Game award were given to Penn State players. The Nittany Lions defeated Washington State 35–28.

Although Penn State was favored to win the 2019 Citrus Bowl, the University of Kentucky Wildcats edged past the Nittany Lions with a 27–24 victory.

The Coaches

There have been **16 head coaches** in Penn State's history.

The Nittany Lions have had three winning seasons since 2014 under head coach James Franklin.

Since its earliest days, Penn State has had many great coaches. The coaches are as important to the team as the players because they shape the way the team plays. Some coaches have led the Lions for a season, while others coached for decades. Five Penn State coaches have been named to the College Football **Hall of Fame**.

BOB HIGGINS In 1914, Bob Higgins started playing football at Penn State as a student and captained the team in 1919. Higgins returned to Penn State in 1930, this time as a coach. In 1947, Higgins took Penn State to the Cotton Bowl. It was the team's second bowl game, and the Nittany Lions tied Southern Methodist University 13–13. The tie ended Penn State's seventh unbeaten season in team history. Higgins left Penn State in 1948.

CHARLES A. "RIP" ENGLE Rip Engle coached the Nittany Lions for 16 seasons from 1950 to 1965. He had a record of 104–48–4 over the course of his career. The Lions played in four bowl games and won three of them under his leadership. The team was also awarded the **Lambert-Meadowlands Trophy** three times under Engle. He was **inducted** into the Pro Football Hall of Fame in 1973.

JAMES FRANKLIN On January 11, 2014, Penn State named James Franklin its new head football coach. He became Penn State's first African American football coach. Franklin has coached Penn State to a bowl game every year since he was hired. His overall record as coach of the Nittany Lions is 45–20. Penn State is Franklin's second head coaching position.

The Mascot

Students who interview to become Nittany Lion must be able to do 50 one-armed push-ups and perform an original two-minute skit. The student chosen to portray the mascot commits to the role for his or her remaining time at Penn State and receives a scholarship, textbooks, and team apparel.

In 1904, Penn State was playing a baseball game against Princeton University. The Princeton team showed the Penn State players a statue of its own mascot, a Bengal tiger. At that moment, Harrison D. "Joe" Mason, a baseball player for Penn State, invented a mascot for the school. Nittany Mountain overlooks Penn State, and mountain lions used to roam its peaks. Mason announced that the Nittany Lion, the "fiercest beast of them all," would defeat the tiger. That day, Penn State defeated Princeton's baseball team 9–1.

Over the next few years, the legend of the Nittany Lion grew. In 1907, it was accepted as Penn State's official mascot, even though it is not a real animal. In 1940, the graduating class gifted the university a stone statue of a mountain lion. It was completed in 1942. Since the early 1920s, a student has dressed in a mountain lion costume and interacted with fans at games. Known simply as "Nittany Lion," it wears a blue-and-white-striped Penn State scarf.

During the annual "Guard the Lion Shrine" event, students and alumni gather around the statue for games, food, live music, and photos with the statue before the homecoming game.

Legends of the Past

For many players, their time with the Nittany Lions is the start of a promising football career. These are some of the best-known football players to play for Penn State.

Mike Michalske

Mike Michalske was known as "Iron Mike" because he was rarely injured. Coach Hugo Bezdek moved him from guard to fullback during the 1925 season. Michalske quickly became a top scorer for Penn State. He won three National Football League (NFL) titles with the Green Bay Packers in 1929, 1930, and 1931. During his time with the Packers, Michalske wore nine different jersey numbers, the most of any NFL player ever. Although an injury stopped him from playing after 1938, he coached for many years after that. In 1964, Michalske became the first guard to be inducted into the Pro Football Hall of Fame.

Position: Fullback/Guard
Seasons: 1923–1925 (Penn State Nittany Lions), 1927–1928 (New York Yankees), 1929–1937 (Green Bay Packers)
Born: April 24, 1903, Cleveland, Ohio

Franco Harris played for Penn State from 1969 to 1971 on a football scholarship. During that time, he rushed 2,002 yards and scored 25 touchdowns. Harris was the first pick for the Pittsburgh Steelers in the 1972 NFL **draft**. In his first year playing professional football, he was part of one of the most famous NFL plays ever. It was called the "Immaculate Reception," and Harris scored a game-winning touchdown against the Oakland Raiders. Harris finished his NFL career in 1984 with 100 total touchdowns, and in 1990, he was inducted into the Pro Football Hall of Fame.

Position: Running Back
Seasons: 1969–1971 (Penn State Nittany Lions), 1972–1983 (Pittsburgh Steelers), 1984 (Seattle Seahawks)
Born: March 7, 1950, Fort Dix, New Jersey

Donovan Smith

Donovan Smith was a well-known left tackle for Penn State. Smith started 31 games with the team. He helped the Nittany Lions rush for 250 or more yards in multiple games and was an All-Big Ten candidate. Smith was selected in the second round of the 2015 NFL draft for the Tampa Bay Buccaneers. He has started all 48 games of his professional career, and in 2015, was named to the NFL All-Rookie Team. During his time with the Tampa Bay Buccaneers, Smith has become an important and reliable part of the team.

Position: Offensive Tackle
Seasons: 2012–2014 (Penn State Nittany Lions), 2015–Present (Tampa Bay Buccaneers)
Born: June 23, 1993, Hempstead, New York

Anthony Zettel

During Anthony Zettel's first three years at Penn State, he appeared in every game with the team. By the time he left the school, he was tied for number of career sacks in Penn State history, with 20. In 2016, Zettel was drafted into the NFL by the Detroit Lions. The next year, Zettel started all 16 games for the Lions. During his time with the team, he had 6.5 sacks and 31 solo tackles. He transferred to the Cleveland Browns in 2018.

Position: Defensive End
Seasons: 2012–2015 (Penn State Nittany Lions), 2016–2017 (Detroit Lions), 2018–Present (Cleveland Browns)
Born: August 9, 1992, Tawas City, Michigan

All-Time Records

8,457

Career Passing Yards

Quarterback Christian Hackenberg holds the Penn State record for passing yards, with 8,457 from 2013 to 2015.

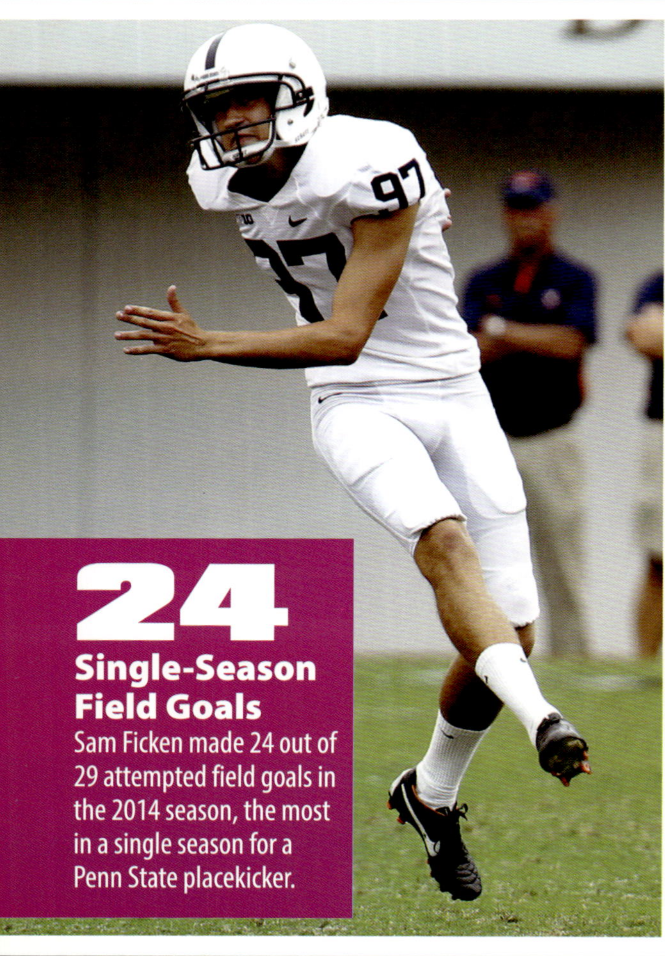

24

Single-Season Field Goals

Sam Ficken made 24 out of 29 attempted field goals in the 2014 season, the most in a single season for a Penn State placekicker.

110,823

Largest Crowd

The largest crowd at Beaver Stadium was 110,823 on October 21, 2017.

419

Career Tackles

Linebacker Dan Connor recorded 227 solo tackles and 192 assisted tackles from 2004 to 2007. His career total of 419 tackles is a Penn State record.

423

Career Points

Kevin Kelly, who played from 2005 to 2008, scored 423 points, the most of any Penn State player.

Timeline

Throughout the team's history, the Penn State Nittany Lions have had many memorable events that have become defining moments for the team and its fans.

1887
Penn State plays its first official football game on November 12, defeating the Bucknell University Bison 54–0.

1905
Penn State wins 73–0 over the Geneva College Golden Tornadoes on November 3, setting a new scoring record.

1907
An article is released recommending that Penn State adopt the lion as its mascot. Later, students vote to make the Nittany Lion their official mascot.

On January 2, 1915, Dick Harlow is named head coach. He is the first former Penn player to be the official head coach.

1900 1920 1940 1960

1941
Dave and Harry Alston become the first African American players on the Penn State team.

1954
Penn State plays its first nationally televised game.

1974
Penn State wins its 500th game.

The Future

The Nittany Lions have been a fixture on the college football scene since they began playing in 1887. Many of their star players have gone on to fame after joining NFL teams. In 2017, James Franklin signed a deal with Penn State to stay on as head coach for another six years. With his successful track record as coach, he will surely lead the team into a bright future.

1983

Penn State unveils a new athletic logo featuring a lion's head on September 9.

2018

Penn State is the top team in the Big Ten East Division and wins its 31st Lambert-Meadowlands Trophy on January 29.

1980

2000

2020

1978

Penn State is voted number-one for the first time in Associated Press polls.

On January 3, 2006, the Nittany Lions win their fourth Orange Bowl in a triple-overtime defeat of the Florida State University Seminoles.

Write a Biography

Life Story

A person's life story can be the subject of a book. This kind of book is called a biography. Biographies often describe the lives of people who have achieved great success. These people may be alive today, or they may have lived many years ago. Reading a biography can help you learn more about a great person.

Get the Facts

Use this book, and research in the library and on the internet, to find out more about your favorite player. Learn as much about him as you can. What position does he play? What are his statistics in important categories? Has he set any records? Also, be sure to write down key events in the person's life. What was his childhood like? What has he accomplished off the field? Is there anything else that makes this person special or unusual?

Use the Concept Web

A concept web is a useful research tool. Read the questions in the concept web on the following page. Answer the questions in your notebook. Your answers will help you write a biography.

Concept Web

Adulthood
- Where does this individual currently reside?
- Does he have a family?

Your Opinion
- What did you learn from the books you read in your research?
- Would you suggest these books to others?
- Was anything missing from these books?

Childhood
- Where and when was this person born?
- Describe his parents, siblings, and friends.
- Did he grow up in unusual circumstances?

Write a Biography

Accomplishments off the Field
- What is this person's life's work?
- Has he received awards or recognition for accomplishments?
- How have this person's accomplishments served others?

Help and Obstacles
- Did this individual have a positive attitude?
- Did he receive help from others?
- Did this person have a mentor?
- Did this person face any hardships?
- If so, how were the hardships overcome?

Accomplishments on the Field
- What records does this person hold?
- What key games and plays have defined his career?
- What are his stats in categories important to his position?

Work and Preparation
- What was this person's education?
- What was his work experience?
- How does this person work?
- What is the process he uses?

Trivia Time

Take this quiz to test your knowledge of the Penn State Nittany Lions. The answers are printed upside down under each question.

1 When was Penn State's football team founded?

A. 1887

2 Who was the Nittany Lions' very first coach?

A. George Hoskins

3 What is the seating capacity for Beaver Stadium?

A. 106,572

4 What are Penn State's colors?

A. Blue and white

5 What was the average GPA of Penn State student athletes in 2018?

A. 3.15

6 Which bowl game did Penn State debut in on January 1, 1923?

A. The Rose Bowl

7 For how many seasons did Coach Rip Engle lead the Nittany Lions?

A. 16

8 What mountain overlooks Penn State and was once home to many mountain lions?

A. Nittany Mountain

9 Which former Penn State player scored 100 touchdowns in the NFL?

A. Franco Harris

10 What is the record attendance for Beaver Stadium?

A. 110,823

Key Words

defensive: having to do with defending against the opposite team in order to prevent them from scoring points

draft: an annual event where the NFL chooses college football players to be new team members

Hall of Fame: a group of persons judged to be outstanding in a particular sport

inducted: added as an official member of a group

lacrosse: a team sport where a ball is thrown, caught, and carried using a long stick with a piece of netting on one end

Lambert-Meadows Trophy: an award given to the best team in the East Division I Football Bowl Subdivision

offensive: having to do with attacking the opposite team in order to score points

postseason: a sporting event that takes place after the end of the regular season

rivals: groups or individuals who compete toward the same objective or goal

traditions: customs or beliefs that are passed from one generation to another

Index

Log on to www.av2books.com

AV² by Weigl brings you media enhanced books that support active learning. Go to www.av2books.com, and enter the special code found on page 2 of this book. You will gain access to enriched and enhanced content that supplements and complements this book. Content includes video, audio, weblinks, quizzes, a slideshow, and activities.

AV² Online Navigation

Audio
Listen to sections of the book read aloud.

Book Pages
AV² pages directly correspond to pages in the book.

Video
Watch informative video clips.

Embedded Weblinks
Gain additional information for research.

Key Words
Study vocabulary, and complete a matching word activity.

Try This!
Complete activities and hands-on experiments.

Quizzes
Test your knowledge.

Slideshow
View images and captions, and prepare a presentation.

AV² was built to bridge the gap between print and digital. We encourage you to tell us what you like and what you want to see in the future.

Sign up to be an AV² Ambassador at www.av2books.com/ambassador.

Due to the dynamic nature of the internet, some of the URLs and activities provided as part of AV² by Weigl may have changed or ceased to exist. AV² by Weigl accepts no responsibility for any such changes. All media enhanced books are regularly monitored to update addresses and sites in a timely manner. Contact AV² by Weigl at 1-866-649-3445 or av2books@weigl.com with any questions, comments, or feedback.